Henry Morris Nixdorff

Life of Whittier's Heroine, Barbara Fritchie

Including a brief but comprehensive sketch of historic. Second Edition

Henry Morris Nixdorff

Life of Whittier's Heroine, Barbara Fritchie
Including a brief but comprehensive sketch of historic. Second Edition

ISBN/EAN: 9783337038793

Printed in Europe, USA, Canada, Australia, Japan

Cover: Foto ©ninafisch / pixelio.de

More available books at **www.hansebooks.com**

LIFE OF

WHITTIER'S HEROINE,

BARBARA FRITCHIE.

INCLUDING A

BRIEF BUT COMPREHENSIVE SKETCH

—OF—

HISTORIC "OLD FREDERICK,"

BY HENRY M. NIXDORFF.

SECOND EDITION.

FREDERICK, MD. :
Great Southern Ptg. & Mfg. Co., Printers and Publishers,
1897.

JOHN G. WHITTIER.

BARBARA FRITCHIE.

Babara Fritchie.

BY JOHN G. WHITTIER.

Up from the meadows rich with corn,
Clear in the cool September morn,

The clustered spires of Frederick stand
Green-walled by the hills of Maryland.

Round about them orchards sweep,
Apple and peach-tree fruited deep,

Fair as a garden of the Lord
To the eyes of the famished rebel horde,

On that pleasant morn of the early Fall
When Lee marched over the mountain-wall,—

Over the mountains winding down,
Horse and foot, into Frederick town.

Forty flags with their silver stars,
Forty flags with their crimson bars,

Flapped in the morning wind : the sun
Of noon looked down, and saw not one.

Up rose old Barbara Fritchie then,
Bowed with her fourscore years and ten:

Bravest of all in Frederick town,
She took up the flag the men hauled down;

In her attic-window the staff she set,
To show that one heart was loyal yet.

Up the street came the rebel tread,
Stonewall Jackson riding ahead.

Under his slouched hat left and right
He glanced; the old flag met his sight.

"Halt!"—the dust-brown ranks stood fast,
"Fire!"—out blazed the rifle-blast.

It shivered the window, pane and sash;
It rent the banner with seam and gash.

Quick, as it fell, from the broken staff
Dame Barbara snatched the silken scarf;

She leaned far out on the window sill,
And shook it forth with a royal will.

"Shoot, if you must, this old gray head,
But spare your country's flag," she said.

A shade of sadness, a blush of shame,
Over the face of the leader came;

The nobler nature within him stirred
To life at that woman's deed and word;

"Who touches a hair of yon gray head
Dies like a dog! March on!" he said.

All day long through Frederick street
Sounded the tread of marching feet;

BARBARA FRITCHIE.

All day long that free flag tost
Over the heads of the rebel host.

Ever its torn folds rose and fell
On the loyal winds that loved it well;

And through the hill-gaps sunset light
Shone over it a warm good-night.

Barbara Fritchie's work is o'er,
And the Rebel rides on his raids no more.

Honor to her! and let a tear
Fall, for her sake, on Stonewall's bier.

Over Babara Fritchie's grave
Flag of Freedom and Union, wave!

Peace and order and beauty draw
Round thy symbol of light and law;

And ever the stars above look down
On thy stars below in Frederick town!

PREFACE.

AS much that is utterly false has been published concerning my friend and neighbor, Mrs. Barbara Fritchie, since the appearance of the wonderful poem entitled "Barbara Fritchie," by that great and justly distinguished poet John G. Whittier, I deem it a duty, as one who loved her, for the many excellent traits of character that she possessed, as well as having been for many years her friend and well acquainted with her for a long time, to tell the public what I know of this worthy lady. The object I have in view, is not to produce anything sensational, or to distort, but to be careful, on the contrary, to make no statement that does not rest on a sure foundation, and I wish it understood that I shall give the exact truth in what I state in the following pages.

The German spelling of Fritchie would be "Freitchie," but we give the English as it was spelled on his small sign at the window where he was conducting business, "Fritchie."

LIFE OF

WHITTIER'S HEROINE,

"BARBARA FRITCHIE."

⤙⤚

MRS. SOUTHWORTH, the distinguished authoress, who was in Washington at the time, was the person who wrote to the poet concerning this estimable lady and enclosed a newspaper slip relating to Barbara Fritchie's action, when Gen. Lee's Army entered Frederick, and this led to the preparation by the poet of that wonderful poem.

Miss Barbara Hauer, was born in the flourishing city of Lancaster, Pennsylvania, December 3d, 1766, and was baptized by the Rev. William Hendel, pastor of the Reformed Church, December 14th, 1766. Her parents names are recorded in the records of the First Reformed Church of Lancaster City, as Nicolas and Catherine Hauer. The names of their five children were Daniel, George, Barbara, Margaret and Catherine. After marriage they were Mrs. John C. Fritchie, Mrs. Stover and Mrs. Peter Mantz. Her husband had received the military title of major and was well known as Major Peter Mantz.

Attention is called at this point for a few moments to Mr. John C. Fritchie the much esteemed husband of our heroine. He was a highly respected citizen of Frederick. His humble and unobtrusive manner won for him the regard of his fellow-citizens, and such is ever the case. True merit is retiring and unassuming.

He conducted a glove manufactory in the east front room of his dwelling, and also prepared the material in his shop fronting on Carroll Creek.

His assistant in the glove department was Mr. Henry Hanshew, who had married Mrs. Fritchie's niece, an honorable man, against whom nothing of evil could be justly spoken.

Mr. Fritchie was successful in business. While he did not acquire great wealth, he accumulated sufficient to live comfortably during life, and at his death, leave to his beloved wife the dwelling in which they had so long resided and means otherwise invested. His death occurred Nov. 10th, 1849. Gone but not forgotten, for beautiful myrtle yet covers his grave.

Miss Barbara Hauer was born in exciting times, when the Colonies of America were still subject to England and stirring events were constantly transpiring.

Just previous to her birth the odious "stamp act," ordering that all papers on which instruments of writing were prepared should be taxed, at exorbitant rates, had been repealed and shortly after, May 1767, a second plan for taxing the colonists was adopted, while yet they were without representation in Parliament. This led to the preparation of that matchless paper "The Declaration of Independence," where each pledged his life, his honor and his fortune, in furtherance of this glorious cause.

The Declaration of Independence and asserting our freedom from British rule, was adopted some ten years after the birth of Miss Barbara Hauer. She was therefore one of those people of hardy origin, who dared to do or die. She no doubt soon learned of the action taken by the citizens of Frederick-town, Maryland, in opposition to British oppression.

As early as 1765 in the old court house in Frederick was the obnoxious "stamp act" pronounced inoperative. And as early in the struggle for our right as 1775, when the battles of Lexington and Bunker Hill aroused the colonies to the succor of Massachusetts, two companies marched from Frederick-town for camp at Boston.

Our heroine was well informed in regard to, and quite conversant, with many events that transpired during the Revolutionary war, and knew full well at how great a sacrifice our national liberty had been obtained. Wonder not then that she stood firm as a rock in defence of her beloved country's best interests, now asserting its just rights.

By a long life of honesty and industry, Mrs. Fritchie enjoyed an honorable and enviable position in society. Therefore if defamer or wicked persons speak ought against her it will only cause her character to shine forth with more resplendent lustre.

Patrick street in Frederick City is one of the principal streets, and extends East and West. The City Hotel on this street has within the last few years been greatly enlarged and improved, and ranks now as a first-class hotel; during the war it was used as a hospital, many who were wounded at the battle of Antietam, after being temporarily lodged at Boonsboro, were brought in ambulances to this hotel. One who held the lantern when they arrived, (for it was night,) said that he was obliged to call some one to take his place, for he was about fainting, he said when he saw them lift one out without an arm, and another with his foot cut off, or the entire limb removed, and noticed their features all distorted with pain, and yet not a murmur escaping their lips, it was more than he could bear. Within the last two years the Electric Railroad has been built passing through the entire street, with cars running from Frederick to Middletown, eight miles distant, almost every hour of the day. Taking the cars on

East Patrick street you can visit the Agricultural Park where the German Baptists held their recent annual meeting attended by large numbers, and by taking the cars on West Patrick you can visit Braddock heights, quite a popular Summer Resort, about four miles west of Frederick.

Mrs. Fritchie's residence was on West Patrick street. It was built of brick and very substantial. It was not large, but neat; one story and a half in height, with two front doors, and three windows in front, beside two dormer windows on the roof. It was painted red and penciled in white, and the shutters were never painted other than pure white. Her home will easily be recognized on the illustrated page, which shows also Carroll creek and the adjoining buildings. The dormer window was at that time quite in style, now they are scarcely seen. Houses that were considered neat and beautiful years ago, are now thought to be quite ordinary.

At one of those dormer windows, I have frequently noticed her standing with her country's flag floating gracefully and beautifully from the same window.

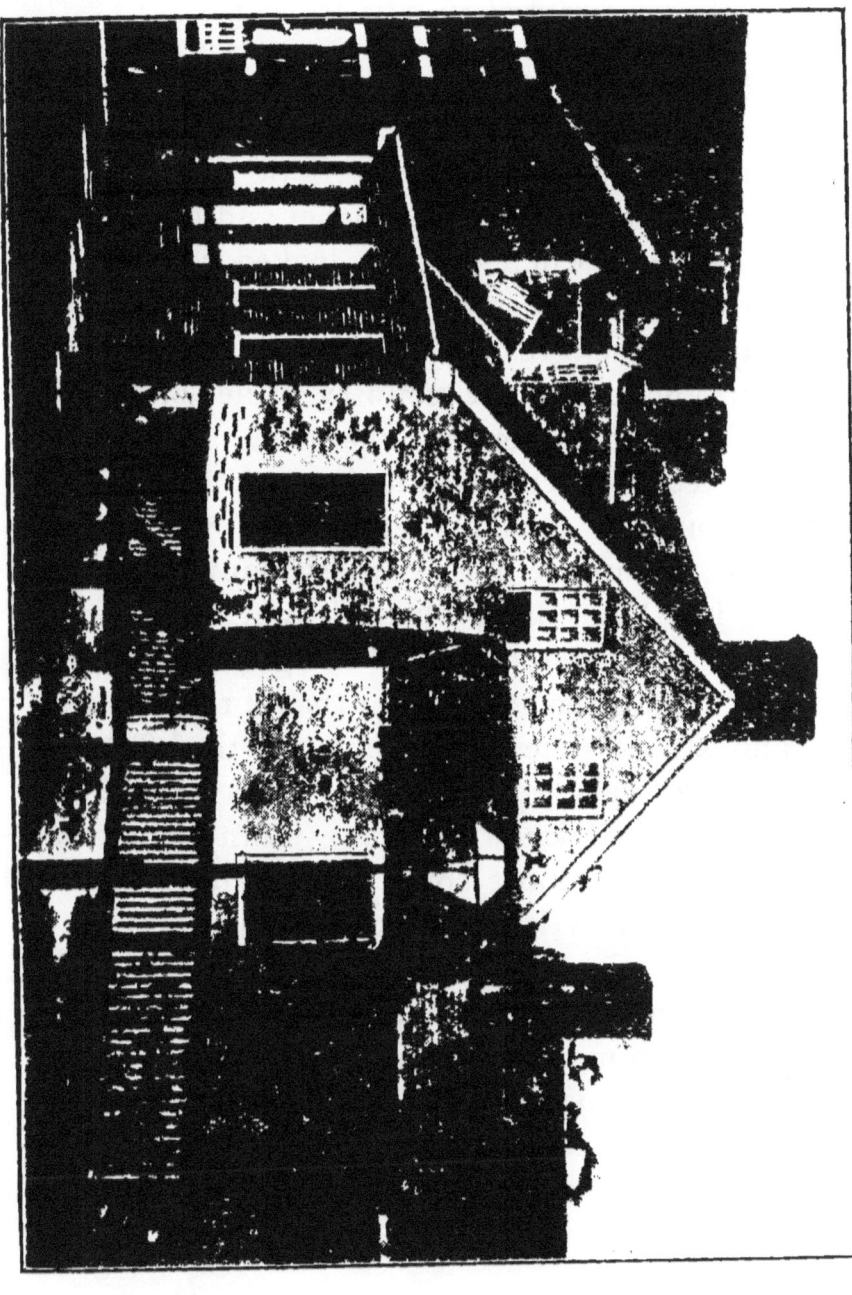

BARBARA FRITCHIE'S HOUSE.

In the early days of the rebellion, when one disaster after another had befallen the Union army, and other patriotic hearts were almost overwhelmed with grief and beginning to despond; when matters looked so dark, so portentous, she stood entirely unmoved, displaying the greatest composure imaginable. Her loyalty to the country of her birth was of the most pronounced character. She never suffered that country to be spoken of in her presence in a disparaging way, without at once, and in the most earnest manner, resenting it. Yes, those small bright eyes would flash with excitement and indignation and her usual calmness, change to that of resoluteness and strong determination, until the offensive remark was recalled, which was invariably done, for all knew that she meant what she said in her inmost soul. She realized that in "Union there is Strength," and believed it with her whole heart.

I shall never forget her appearance as she came into my store during the earlier part of the war, leaning on her staff and saying with the greatest earnestness, "Do not for a moment despair, stand firm."

Often when she entered the store, she would ask, "How do matters look now for the Union side?" Sometimes I had just heard good news of a cheering character, and when I would communicate it to her, joy was manifested in the most fervent manner. Her whole frame kindled with emotion and her bright eyes sparkled with delight. At other times news of a saddening character had been received, and when I made it known to her I felt greatly depressed. She would notice it at once and remark, "O, do not be cast down, it will all come right, I know it will, the Union must be preserved," and remark with the greatest emphasis, "Be assured that God takes care of his people, and he will take care of this country. I feel perfectly satisfied that the Union of the States will be maintained. I am sure that it is God's will that the Union shall continue and you know that nothing can stand against that." Thus it was that encouragement was given by this patriotic lady when many strong men became lukewarm and indifferent, and even when the Flag of the land that gave them birth was ruthlessly assailed. Although more than thirty years have elapsed since that time, yet that aged form, that feeble step, I never can, never shall forget. She was one of those persons who impress you favorably at the first interview, and that impression strengthens as time rolls on. I loved her, though aged and weak, and treasure up as precious the words I heard her speak. If her Country did wrong she would not forsake, but endeavor to place her in the right. True, she had lived more than ninety years of pleasure, pain, toil and tears, but it only made her attachment take deeper root for the cause of her Country, the cause of truth. Yes, she loved this blessed land of lands, upon which Heaven has showered its richest blessings. She had great will power, and such persons accomplish most in this world, although in the political arena women can do but little, not having the right to express sentiments through the ballot box; yet by well directed efforts and influence in certain directions she has already accomplished much. Look, for instance, at what has been done by the Womans' Christian Temperance Union for the cause of humanity!

Mrs. Fritchie was not robust, but decision

of character was seen throughout, and judging from her eyes and mouth she surely was not one to be trifled with. If she said, No! it was quite plain that she was settled in the opinion formed, and to change it was no easy task, for when formed aright it was formed to last. In conversation she was quite refined, her language was always chaste, entirely pure; thus setting an example which was no doubt the means of leading many in the right direction. Persons calling on her were sure to meet with a kind, cordial welcome. Carroll Creek, a small stream, flowed past the gable-end of her back building on its way to the Monocacy. At one of the windows that looked out upon the creek I have frequently, on my way to the Spring, now known as "City Spring," noticed her sitting, either sewing, knitting, or reading some favorite book, always busily engaged in doing something. It is not to be wondered at therefore, that she understood household duties, or that she could converse intelligently upon almost any subject. As a wife she was thoroughly domestic and by her genial disposition and well stored mind made home what it ever should be—a happy, lovable and attractive

place.   To so great an extent was this the case
that her beloved husband was seldom absent
from it when the evening shades gathered
around.   Thus happy, thus joyous, could every
home be made.

She was the senior of her husband by a
number of years.   I have frequently heard my
mother remark that a company of young ladies
were present at a quilting party, when it was
announced that a son had been born to Mrs.
Fritchie.   Among the young ladies attending
the party was the beautiful and accomplished
Miss Barbara Hauer, who in the course of time
became the beloved and devoted wife of Mr.
John C. Fritchie whose birth it was that was
announced that night.   I do not suppose that
our heroine ever weighed over 110 or 115
pounds.   She was slight in figure and scarcely
of medium height, her eyes were small but
penetrating and keen, her hair was dark in
early life, but at last the silver threads began
to take the place of the dark brown. At length,
having lost much of her hair, she was induced
to purchase a braid, which gave her the appearance of one much younger than she really
was.   In her dress she was remarkable for

plainness, the variations were few indeed. About the house her costume was usually that of plain quaker colored calico, and when she went to the store, or when she visited neighbors or attended church, you could rest assured that she would be clad in a black cashmere or alpaca dress, though she had a handsome

CHINAWARE AND RELICS.

plum colored silk and other costly dresses, which she could have worn. She was a poor visitor, seldom going among her neighbors, and, all things considered, perhaps too much visiting is not to be commended. She possessed much beautiful chinaware. A relative of her's residing in our city has at the present time cups and saucers, teapot and other chinaware, which formerly belonged to Mrs. Fritchie, also gold ear rings and an excellent likeness of her aged relative. Out of the tea pot Gen. George Washington drank tea the night he spent in Frederick, in the year 1791. The way it happened was as follows: The young ladies of the town had a quilting party at Mrs. Kimball's Hotel, where the City Hotel is now located. They entertained Gen. Washington, and Miss Barbara Hauer loaned her chinaware to grace the table. When Gen. Washington died these same young ladies held a sham funeral and our heroine acted as one of the pall bearers. She was not accustomed to speak in a boasting way of any act that she performed, for she considered that when in the discharge of duty she was only doing that which she believed to be right. Therefore she did not understand why a person should be so highly complimented for doing what God's word taught her was the right, and which if she deviated from would be taking a step in the wrong direction. The poor and distressed ever had a sympathising friend in her, and though not able to do or give as much as some others, she did all she could. This is all that is required, for you know it is said in God's blessed word, that if we only give a cup of cold water with the proper spirit to one in need it is pleasing in the sight of our Heavenly Father.

She was benevolent, in the highest sense of the term, not making excuses, as some do, and turning worthy and unworthy persons indiscriminately from her door. I feel assured that plain, unostentatious benevolence is such as is acceptable in Jehovah's sight. She never courted the society of the great and noble of the earth, if pride and wealth alone made them such in the sight of those with whom they associated. She was fond of cultivating flowers. Between the front house and the back building at her residence there was a small triangular parcel of ground. This she had planted with beautiful flowers and very often you might find her at work in this little flower garden. I remember as clearly as though it were but yesterday of frequently standing on the bridge adjoining and viewing the lovely roses, dahlias, chrysanthemums, as well as other flowers blooming in this little bed. I cannot forget

in the dry goods trade in Frederick City, and of course we had to bear considerable loss. Having a large country trade, we kept besides the regular goods, boots, shoes, hats and caps. I do not think that I shall ever forget how I felt when three Confederate soldiers came into the store and asked me,—when I was alone— to show them some shoes and then asked the price. They were the first Southern soldiers I had met or seen. I handed the shoes down from the shelves. Two pair were each priced $1.50, the other pair $1.75. They said, "We will take the three pair." I wrapped them up, when one of the soldiers handed me a $20.00 Confederate note and waited for the change. You can easily imagine the dilemma I was in. I would not give him change in United States money, and therefore gave him the note back, which amused them all very much. They picked up the package of shoes and went out and away. I looked around and saw that the store was getting crowded with soldiers, in front, back of the counter and everywhere. Of course one or two of us could do nothing. If we could have waited on them they would have been willing to pay with such money as they had, and some of them did hand a ten or twenty dollar Confederate note and took shoes, boots and hats to the full amount. The majority, however, would throw the boots and shoes across their arms and move off without saying a word, even my own hat and boots kept for occasional wear were taken. When the Confederate army, led by Generals Lee, Jackson and others, entered Frederick City, on Saturday morning, September 6, 1862, it is said that as they came marching up East Patrick street Gen. Jackson was in command, at least for some time. It is certain that their appearance did not occasion the uprising of the people that the Confederate Generals had been led to expect from a people who were thought to be down-trodden and oppressed. Many of those, even, who were thought to be in sympathy with them did not open their doors to welcome them. On Monday, September 8th, Gen. Lee issued his proclamation to the people of Maryland calling on them to throw off the restraint of the Union Government and join the South. A general uprising of the people was no doubt expected to result from the invitation, which, however, did not receive the slightest response.   The following is the proclamation:

HEADQUARTERS ARMY N. VA., }
Near Frederick Town, Sept. 8, 1862. }

To THE PEOPLE OF MARYLAND:

It is right that you should know the purpose that has brought the army under my command within the limits of your State, so far as that purpose concerns yourselves.

The people of the Confederate States have long watched with the deepest sympathy the wrongs and outrages that have been inflicted upon the citizens of a Commonwealth allied to the States of the South by the strongest social, political and commercial ties.

They have seen with profound indignation their sister State deprived of every right and reduced to the condition of a conquered province.

Under the pretense of supporting the Constitution, but in violation of its most valuable provisions, your citizens have been arrested and imprisoned upon no charge and contrary to all forms of law; the faithful and manly protest against this outrage, made by the venerable and illustrious Marylander to whom in better days no citizen appealed for right in vain, was treated with scorn and contempt.   The government of your city has been usurped by armed strangers; your Legislature been dissolved by the unlawful arrest of its members; freedom of the press and speech have been suppressed; words have been declared offences by an arbitrary decree of the Federal executive and citizens ordered to be tried by a military commission for what they may dare to speak. Believing that the people of Maryland possessed a spirit too lofty to submit to such a government, the people of the South have long wished to aid you in throwing off this foreign yoke, to enable you to again enjoy the inalienable rights of freemen and restore independency and sovereignty to your State.

In obedience to this wish our army has come among you and is prepared to assist you with the power of its arms in regaining the rights of which you have been despoiled.

This, citizens of Maryland is our mission, so far as yourselves are concerned. No restraint upon your free will is intended; no intimidation will be allowed within the limits of this army, at least Marylanders shall once more enjoy their ancient freedom of thought and speech.

We know of no enemies among you, and will protect all of every opinion. It is for you to decide your destiny, freely and without restraint.

This army will respect your choice whatever it may be, and while the Southern people will rejoice to welcome you to your natural position among them, they will only welcome you when you come of your own free will.

R. E. LEE, Commanding.

To General Lee's great surprise his proclamation created no enthusiasm whatever, but fell entirely harmless, gaining nothing in the way of aid or comfort, but on the contrary intensifying the feeling of loyalty and devotion to the Union. In the language of Col. J. Thomas Scharf in his history of Western Maryland, "The reception of the Confederate troops, by the inhabitants of Frederick, was decidedly cool. Not the slightest manifestation of joy and enthusiasm was exhibited. With all places of business closed and the streets deserted by the people, the old town wore a gloomy appearance in striking contrast to the resplendency displayed, upon the entry of the Union army one week later.

On Wednesday morning, Sept. 10th, 1862, the Confederate army began to move out of Frederick city.

General Jackson's corps was in the advance. As they passed out West Patrick street, I stood at the front window of my dwelling, looking at regiment after regiment, clad in grey or brown uniforms, as they marched past for several hours. So intent was I in noticing and reflecting on this lamentable action on the part of the people against the best government on earth that I lost sight of what was going on at Mrs. Fritchie's, although her residence was not a square distant from my own. But this I do believe, that if the opportunity was presented she did not fail to improve it, for I do not think that she would have taken a backward step though confronted by their entire army. In the language of Mrs. Abbott, "Aunt Fritchie was fearless and very patriotic." A single incident will show the spirit animating her. On one occasion a number of Confederate soldiers halted and sat down on the porch in front of her dwelling, and were drinking water brought from the spring near by. To this she had not the least objection, but before leaving they began to speak in a derogatory manner of her beloved country. In a moment she arose and passing to the front door she bade them clear themselves and applied the "cane," with which she used to walk, in the most vigorous manner, clearing the porch in a few moments of every man upon it. I am inclined to believe from enquiry that General Jackson on the day the Confederates passed through Frederick, did not pass by the dwelling of Mrs. Fritchie. It appears that he left his soldiers, at the East end of the city, to call on the Rev. Dr. John B. Ross, pastor of the Presbyterian church, the wife of whom was the daughter of Ex-Gov. McDowell, of Virginia, with whom he was well acquainted. It being early in the morning it is declared that he wrote the following note, and slipped it under the front door at Dr. Ross's dwelling.

REV. JOHN B. ROSS :—

Regret not being able to see you and Mrs. Ross, but could not expect to have that pleasure at so unseasonable an hour.

T. J. JACKSON.

Dr. Ross resided on West Second street, and it is stated that Gen. Jackson on leaving Dr. Ross's residence rode on to what is known as Bentz street and rejoined his soldiers by coming up a portion of Bentz street, commonly called "Mill Alley," which leads out into Pat-

PRESBYTERIAN PARSONAGE.

rick street a short distance beyond or on the West side of Mrs. Fritchie's residence. I measured the distance from " Mill Alley" to her dwelling and found it 63 yards. Grant that it was not Gen. Jackson, might it not have been some other officer in command, if so it would not change the principle involved. I have, however, no personal knowledge of its occurrence. This I do know; called for a moment to my front door that morning to see a friend, I happened to look up the street, and saw a very intelligent lady, a neighbor, standing on her front porch, with a small United States flag in her hand waving it and making apparently the most earnest remarks to a Confederate officer who had ridden his horse over on the pavement up to the porch where she was standing. I was afterward assured by those who had the pleasure of being present that such glowing words of patriotism fell from the lips of Mrs. Quantrell that the officer looked on and listened with wonder and surprise, and whilst he was present would not allow his men do her the least harm. After his departure, however, some of the soldiers belonging to the army came and knocked the flag from her hand, breaking the staff into several pieces.

In order to corroborate what I had written I addressed the following note to Mr. Fleming, and all his brothers and sisters joined in attesting to its correctiveness.

Mr. WILLIAM W. FLEMING:—

Esteemed friend, will you please give me the information that I desire if it is in your power to do so. When some years since the Confederate army passed through Frederick city, it is said that your neighbor at that time, Mrs. Mary Quantrell, stood on the porch in front of her house and waved a small United States flag, and that a Confederate officer rode up to the porch and remonstrated with her for doing so, and urged her to desist, whereupon she spoke to him in such glowing words of patriotism that he was quite astonished, listening to her most respectfully, and whilst he was present would not allow her to be disturbed; that after his departure soldiers belonging to the army came up and knocked the flag out of her hand several times, breaking the flag staff. Is the foregoing correct ? By answering the questions propounded you will greatly oblige Your friend,

H. M. NIXDORFF.

We, the undersigned, find the foregoing statement to be correct.

Mrs. Matilda Fleming,
Mrs. Hallie M. McDonald,
Mrs. Kate H. Cashour,
Nicholas H. Fleming,
Wm. W. Fleming.

If this occurred at Mrs. Mary Quantrell's we should not be astonished at anything said to have taken place at another point.

On the 12th of September Gen. McClellan's army entered Frederick city. The advance was under command of Gen. Burnside. As they moved up West Patrick street on the National pike leading westward, they passed Mrs. Fritchie's residence. She was standing at one of the front windows of her dwelling, leaning on her cane. Beside her stood her relative, Miss Julia Hanshew, now Mrs. John H. Abbott; and Miss Yoner. As she stood by the window she waved her hand time and again to express her joy. Miss Yoner, no doubt at Mrs. Fritchie's request, went into the adjoining room and brought forth Mrs. Fritchie's flag. The old lady grasped it and stood at the window waving it. As she waved her

MRS. QUANTRELL'S HOUSE.

flag the soldiers were perfectly delighted, some of them loudly cheering her, others ran to the window and as soon as they could get near enough grasped her by the hand and said "God bless you, old lady, may you live long, you dear old soul." And then cheer after cheer was given as our noble soldiers marched along. That same silk flag I have had in my hands only a short time since. Among those who shook hands with her that day was the beloved and valiant Gen. Reno.

It has been said truthfully, that the sun never shone upon a more patriotic people during those trying times, than the loyal Union men and women of the South, of which type our heroine was a distinguished example. She had early secured a United States flag, and often during the earlier part of the rebellion when matters looked dark and threatening to the Union army, I have seen that glorious emblem of our country's honor floating from the dormer window of her house, and my old neighbor standing beside the flag-staff looking intently at that which is the symbol of freedom, equality before the law, and the just rights of mankind wherever unfurled. A consecrated,

blessed emblem. Thousands upon thousands
have laid down their lives in its defense, and
if required in the future, myriads would step
forth to do the same thing, willing to die that
the old flag might still wave.

Three miles southeast of Frederick City
the battle of the Monocacy River was fought.
The Union soldiers were of Gen. Tyler's division and under command of Gen. Lewis
Wallace. They fought valiantly but were finally
repulsed by the enemy, who were in superior
numbers, after many had been slain and
wounded on both sides. As the Union army
withdrew they set fire to and burned the large
wooden bridge spanning the Monocacy at this
point, so that the Confederates, who were on
the western bank of the river, found it more
difficult to pursue them. Some seventeen miles
westward from Frederick City the battle of
South Mountain was fought, September 14,
1862. It was a battle of great interest and
magnitude. The excitement in Frederick was
almost unbounded, for it looked as though our
beloved State of Maryland might become the
central battle ground between the North and
the South, and our citizens be called upon to

witness terrible scenes. Happily, this was averted, but many of our people nevertheless suffered severely by having their property taken from them at different periods, particularly by the raids of the enemy. As General McClellan's army or division was moving on the National pike, leading westward, they had several skirmishes with the enemy. The one on Catoctin mountain was quite severe, lasting however, only a short time. The discharge of the musketry could be heard distinctly in Frederick. The battle of South Mountain was a decided victory for the Union side. It was with saddened hearts, however, that we learned that in the engagement the brave and noble Gen. Reno, who only a few days previous had grasped the venerable Mrs. Fritchie by the hand, lost his life whilst worthily discharging his duty.

As I have said much in favor of our aged heroine, you might possibly suppose that I regarded her as perfect. Now this would be an incorrect conclusion, for I am well aware that we have had but one perfect character in this sin-cursed world, and that was our blessed Lord and Saviour. We do say, however, that

if faults and blemishes did exist—and we do
not for a moment doubt it.—they were un-
known to the writer of these pages. It may
be that her many virtues and excellencies so
completely overshadowed her faults as to ren-
der them undiscoverable to those by whom she
was surrounded. I was conversing recently
with Mr. John Riehl, a neighbor of mine for
many years, and with whom I have been inti-
mately acquainted. He was also for many years
a neighbor of Mrs. Fritchie's. Speaking of our
heroine, he said, that when a boy he was sent
to Mrs. Fritchie's every day for milk, for she
kept a cow for many years. Said Mr. Riehl:
"You know the old lady had a decided way of
speaking." I said, "Yes." "Well," continued
Mr. Riehl, "Sometimes when I would reach
her house the milking had not been completed
and she would say to me, 'Take that small
branch from the tree and keep the flies from
disturbing the cow whilst being milked.' I
quickly did as commanded but always kept an
eye on her, fearing that she might give me a
whipping if I did not do it to please her. After I reached manhood and met her often I

found that she possessed one of the kindest hearts imaginable."

During the days of slavery, long before the war, Mr. and Mrs. Fritchie were the owners of slaves. "Fritchie's Harry" and "Aunt Nellie" were known quite well. "Harry" used to work in the skin dressing department and "Old Aunt Nellie," at the household duties. They were very clever people, and were treated with great kindness by their owners. They in turn, loved "Old Massa" and "Old Missus," insomuch that when Harry was allowed to go and do for himself and live in another part of the town he would be constantly coming back to see "Old Massa" and "Old Missus" up to the time of his death. If the same kind feeling had existed between all owners of slaves, several of the most thrilling chapters in "Uncle Tom's Cabin," by Mrs. Stowe would never have been written in truth.

You will pardon, I feel assured, a digression before proceeding further with the life of our heroine, by calling attention briefly to another remarkable person, a native of Frederick county.

About thirteen miles to the northwest of

Frederick City, is located the former residence of that intelligent Christian hero, George Blessing. He lived his lifetime in Middletown Valley, and bore an irreproachable character. He was known for a considerable distance around for his deeds of valor and heroism. I will give a short account of this distinguished patriot. His library did not consist of a choice collection, culled from the most distinguished authors of the day. No! it consisted of only a few books, but these were of the very best, and were read over and over again. He never became weary of perusing two of them ; his well-worn Bible and the "Lives of American Statesmen." On his countenance firmness was depicted, and his broad forehead indicated sound judgment. His eyes were blue, and in his bosom beat a kind and noble heart. I have a photograph which is a perfect likeness of Mr. Blessing. The orignal was loaned me by one of his near relatives, who prizes it very highly. When the Confederate army came into Maryland, Mr. Blessing's home afforded temporary shelter for those fleeing before the advancing foe. On leaving they always advised him to accompany them, but he invariably re-

fused, saying that he intended to remain and
by God's help protect his home and family. I
have been at his former home since the close
of the war, and it is surely a beautiful and ro-
mantic place. When the battle of South Mountain was being fought the report of the artillery and discharge of the musketry could be
distinctly heard at his residence, known as
"Highlands." He had on hand several old guns
which he had obtained at different periods.
These he commenced cleaning and loading,
with the assistance of his son, Lewis. On the
morning of the 9th of September, news came
that the enemy were approaching the bounda-
ries of his farm. His situation, considering
how strong a Union man he had always been,
was indeed perilous; but he was perfectly
calm and asked his family to engage with
him in prayer, in which he implored the Almighty to protect him and all the beloved
members of his family, and if in accordance
with His will still ' uphold the old flag.
Such scenes make lasting impressions on
those present. He listened not to the en-
treaties of the female portion of his family to
still make his escape. Calling his son Lewis

to take two of the guns, they started for the barn-yard, where they secreted themselves and awaited the approach of the foe. They soon saw a squad of men approaching. The invaders drew near cautiously, and not meeting with opposition one of them dismounted and commenced breaking open the stable door. Mr. Blessing called out in a loud voice, "If you touch that door again you shall surely suffer." They all looked around and gazed in every direction, but were unable to determine from whence the sound came. They looked startled, as though they had heard an unearthly sound. At length they became calm and began their work again. Mr. Blessing and his son fired their guns at the same time upon the intruders. Both balls proved effective. The right arm dropped at the side of one of the men. The balance observing a cross-fire, and believing that a large force was hidden and waiting to be attacked, fled at once, leaving their wounded comrade behind, and loudly declaring that they would return and take revenge on Mr. Blessing and his supporters. As they were retreating Mr. Blessing fired a second shot after them. It entered the back

of one of their number and he fell dead on
the ground. Mr. Blessing took the man that
was wounded to his own home and had his
wounds dressed· As the old hero met his beloved wife he exclaimed, "Praise God, we are
yet safe." His wife, fearing that they might
return in large numbers, once more urged him
to seek refuge in flight, but he said he had
abiding confidence in the true and living God
and therefore stood unmoved. He loaded his
guns once more, and having given orders about
the family not leaving the house, started for
the stable. When he reached that point he
helped to place the body of the dead man in
the stable, subsequently it was buried, and
then waited for the foe. He did not have to
wait long, for soon a number of horsemen
heavily armed came riding down the lane.
When they had gotten near where Mr. Blessing was, three of the men were ordered to go
forward and find out what force the old hero
had at his command with which to oppose
them, and return as soon as possible and report. As they were passing the clump of
trees, Mr. Blessing shouted "halt!" and then
said, "what is your business?" They replied,

"to learn what force you have." Then said
Mr. Blessing, "form into line and cross the
road, and enter into my service, the man diso-
beying will be instantly shot." They did as
commanded. The soldiers in the distance
fired vigorously at Mr. Blessing, and he just
as earnestly returned their fire. They knew
not what to do. At length, believing the old
hero's force to be much larger than it really
was, they concluded to withdraw. As they
wheeled around Mr. Blessing quickly aimed a
shot at the leader of the band and wounded
him severely, for he was seen to fall forward
on his horse's neck, and was hurriedly taken
away by his fellow soldiers. The men whom
he had captured stood almost dumbfounded at
what they had witnessed. On dismissing them
he gave each man his hand, and urged one and
all of them in the most heartfelt manner to
be true in the future to God and his country.
When he reached home, it is impossible to express the joy of his beloved family at receiv-
ing him once more. If they shed tears, if
they threw their arms around and embraced
him, we need not wonder, for his was almost
a miraculous preservation. "Blessed be God,"

he said, "for he has protected and defended me." A third time he reloaded his gun and walked down the lane. It was not long before a large force was seen approaching. Resolving to die, if die he must, with his face to the foe, he came out away from all concealment, and raising his gun, was making ready to fire, when he noticed a white flag waving. What can it mean he thought. It surely must be the sign for a truce. You can readily imagine his joy at discovering as they drew near that instead of enemies they were friends. Cole's Cavalry, who were some distance off, learning of his situation and bravery at once hastened toward his residence to extend all the assistance in their power.

We must now resume the history of our heroine. She enjoyed remarkably good health, scarcely knowing what it was to be sick, until the last, and of course, fatal attack came on, when like a sheaf of wheat, ready to be garnered, she gently and sweetly rested in the arms of her Saviour. Having been clothed with immortal life, she reached that city out of sight whose builder and maker is God. Yes, Mrs. Fritchie at length became enfeebled by age and gathering her robes about her, she calmly waited for the coming of her blessed Lord. He came on that bleak, cold, 18th day of December, 1862. All without was dreary and gloomy, but within that chamber of death there was perfect peace, beautifully exemplifying that passage of Scripture "Those shall rest in perfect peace whose minds are stayed on Him." Life's flickering lamp at length ceased to burn, and as far as this world is concerned, all was over, all had closed. We doubt not but that our aged friend is now enjoying and will forever enjoy raptures of bliss around the throne of God. How precious is such a memory. Ninety some years to God and her country given, and now at home in Heaven. What a glorious thought it is, that after life's cares and anxieties are all over,—and some in passing through this would meet with so much trouble,—we reach at length the New Jerusalem, to go out no more forever. Mrs. Fritchie's remains rest in the Cemetery of the Reformed Church in Frederick City, in a lot enclosed with an iron railing, beside her husband. A neat block of marble has been placed at the head of the grave, and bears the following inscription.

"Barbara Fritchie, died December 18th, 1862. Aged 96 years."

Her age as given me by Mrs. Hanshew, taken from the old family Bible, was 96 years and 15 days. A small block of marble at the foot of the grave, bears the initials "B. F."

BARBARA FRITCHIE'S GRAVE.

The block of marble at the head of her husband's grave is similar to that of his wife's, and reads :

"John C. Fritchie, died November 10th, 1849. Aged 69 years."

The small b'ock at the foot bears the initials "J. C. F." The Cemetery is beautifully

located, somewhat elevated toward the eastern
part, or front, and gradually declining as it
extends westward. It fronts on Bentz street,
at the West end of Second street. On visiting
the Cemetery lately I found a small United
States flag gently waving over her grave. It
needs no storied urn or animated bust to per-
petuate her memory or that of Francis Scott
Key, a Marylander by birth and a native of
this county, whose remains have been depos-
ited in Mount Olivet Cemetery in this city.
And yet I hope that ere long monuments of
an imposing character will be erected to the
memory of these distinguished patriots. Summer in all its beauty may come and go, wintry
winds around us rudely blow, but who shall
know the time when the youthful heart shall
cease to glow at the mention of Barbara Fritchie's name. O, how much from such an example we may learn. It gleams forth at almost
every turn, and one of the leading facts that
we should discern, is, that our hearts should
ever burn with love and devotion to our blessed
country. Any one can speak well of his
country when all is calm and clear, when
naught can do us harm. Who need fear, at

such a time, even an Arnold may appear to hold his country's interest dear and speak in her defense. O, where could baser ingratitude appear, than after enjoying our country's blessings far and near, she should call, and we turn a deaf ear, or be a stumbling block in the way.

May we to our country be firm as a rock or wall, willing for her to stand or fall, ready for her to risk our lives, our all. Such was Barbara Fritchie. Her brothers and sisters have long since passed from this sphere of action. All of them have exchanged time for eternity. Numerous relatives, however, are still living. A son of Mr. Daniel Hauer, relatives of Mrs. Catherine Mantz, children of Mr. George Hauer and the widow of Mr. Henry Hanshew and her children, besides others distantly related, reside in our midst, and are among our very best and most useful citizens. Mr. George Eissler purchased the "Fritchie property," after the decease of our heroine, from the heirs, and conducted the dyeing business at that place for several years. Whilst Mr. Eissler owned the property we were visited by the "great freshet" of July 24th, 1868. The water rose to a great height and washed out a corner of the "Fritchie building." Afterward the corporation of Frederick, from a desire to avoid danger in the future, bought the property from Mr. Eissler and after selling the building as it stood, on the lot from which it was removed in a short time by Mr. James Hopwood the purchaser, the Corporation commenced the work of widening the stream, taking in a portion of the lot, where Mrs. Fritchie formerly resided, and subsequently sold the balance of the lot to Mr. James Hopwood, whose son, James W. Hopwood, purchased it from his father and erected a two-story brick dwelling with store room in front, where he has conducted the tinning business ever since. When the work of removing the building commenced the deep interest felt in our aged deceased neighbor was manifested by many of the citizens gathering around and collecting small bits of wood from doors and window frames. This continued until the gentleman who had purchased the material of the building, announced that he would make a number of canes out of the wood of the window frames and rafters, which were of solid oak, and furnish them to the public at a reasonable price. This he did, and some persons secured several, to present to valued friends as "mementoes." Polished up nicely they presented a very pretty appearance. Meeting a friend with one on the street a short time since I asked him what amount he would take for it. "Oh," said he, "I would not take anything in reason, for I do not know where I could obtain another.

What could rejoice the heart of Mrs. Fritchie more, who has long since reached the "Everlasting City," than looking down from her celestial home (for we believe that the spirits in bliss are cognizant of what is going on in this world,) upon the land she so much loved, and seeing that land growing in wealth and in power; taking her place among the most notable nations on earth in rank and influence. Go on, our native land, may God give us grace to sustain thy free institutions and uphold thy laws. The government of the United States is now acknowledged to be the best on earth by all fair minded people, for here all the officers are elected by and held responsible to the people for all official acts. The various nations of the earth are now treating

with the greatest respect and consideration the
United States, observing that she is rapidly
increasing in population and making great
progress each passing hour in science, art and
agriculture, and it will doubtless continue until we attain to the most complete development
possible.

Our territory is now reaching far and
wide, and we have no doubt but that it is destined some day to include Canada and Cuba.
The worthy emigrant can here secure a home
and become a citizen of this great country. It
is our duty to take such by the hand and show
them that by industry and sobriety they may
attain to high positions of trust and influence,
as well as respectability, and enjoy the rights
and privileges of freemen, such as were un-
known to them in the "Fatherland." But in
order to become such citizens they must endeavor to assimilate with our government and
give their cordial support to all the principles
and laws that have in the past conduced to
make us a great people. A most gratifying
fact to every lover of his country, is, that
twenty-five years have worked wondrous
changes in the minds of the American people,

and many doctrines deemed false and unten-
able at that time are now accepted as truths
and acquiesced in by the great masses of the
people of the United States. And we have the
glorious knowledge that from North to South,
and from East to West, all over this vast do-
main, where heretofore alienation existed, you
now find a spirit of concord and brotherly love
springing up, which is so essential to happiness
and all that renders life enjoyable and enables
us to bear patiently the difficulties with which
we have to contend. It is a blessed thing to
have peace in a family and also in the nation,
doing entirely away with discord and strife
and all ill-nature, especially such evil feelings
as have been engendered by the warfare of one
section of our beloved country against another.
It has to be, however, a gradual work for the
great animosity, yea! genuine hatred, exhibited by one section toward the other can only
be eradicated as time rolls on. It is a blessed
thing to forgive and forget. We rejoice that
the time is hastening on when brother and
friend shall heartily greet each other and let
the dead past be blotted out of remembrance
from one portion of the country to the othe r.

So that, with loving expressions, the Blue and
the Grey, who had engaged in many a desperate conflict on the battle-field, where both displayed great bravery amid most trying scenes,
where the courage of the one or the other was
never questioned, can, laying everything else
aside, once more meet, forgetting, as it were,
past differences, on common ground and feel
that now mutual interest and sympathy exist,
however far assunder they may have been before. How pleasant, how joyful will that time
be. Many are anxiously awaiting the period of
complete restoration of fraternal feeling. Then
will the past be left forever at rest and then
will harmony and good-will once more abound.

What valid reason can be assigned for
keeping up this evil spirit, for all the issues
involved have long since been settled! If we
expect and desire the nation to prosper we
must all work heartily together for its upbuild-
ing, and then success will crown our efforts.
The passions of excited persons may lead them
into great wrong, but a time will come for
sound judgement to assert its sway, and then
matters are viewed in a different light from
what they were before.

During the late war when opposing armies covered the plain and the dull sound of cannon could be heard in Frederick, even from the battle-field at Gettysburg, it is not to be wondered at that excitement ran high, for momentous issues were indeed involved. Mrs. Fritchie amid it all was calm and collected. "What I do thou knowest not now, but shalt know hereafter," saith Jehovah, and our aged friend believed it fully. We one day shall know that what God has done for you, for me, for all, is undoubtedly the best. And yet this is so hard to learn and understand because we want our own way, and are not willing to be led by "infinite wisdom." Mrs. Fritchie believed that God saw that it was best for all the people of this great nation to be free and thus make our Declaration of Independence not a mockery, but true and complete. Free as the air we breathe, yes, free as all would wish to be, for who that has enjoyed liberty, for only a single moment, or day, would wish to be bound in chains again. The union of the States must be held inviolate, must not be disturbed. In it there is strength, there is power. We will be held responsible and will unquestionably have to give account for the influence we have exerted. This free, united country, is yet to do a great work in the evangelization of the world. Who can for a moment doubt, but that the "Star Spangled Banner" will eventually be planted in distant lands where darkness and superstition now reign supreme. Glorious Banner, each star and stripe has been baptized in blood, destined to float, as we believe, from every pinnacle and dome the wide world over, and proving the harbinger of every blessing. May we not hope that the day is not distant when all nations shall enjoy the blessing so long vouchsafed to us. Columbia, thou hast given birth to many of the most distinguished men that have ever lived. Among that number stands the noble Washington, who, at the close of his term of service as President of the United States, when he might have proclaimed himself, or been declared Emperor of the people, quietly laid aside the insignia of office and became a private citizen. What a noble course was this pursued by the beloved Father of his Country. Civil and religious liberty has been fully established in the United States, to continue, we hope, as long as the world shall stand.

We would not interfere with the powers that be, but we do believe that ere many years shall have rolled around tyrants and despots will learn that their reign must cease. When we think of Sixteen Hundred and Twenty, when this land was a wilderness, inhabited by savages and wild beasts, how dismal and gloomy was the scene presented. It was enough to cause the heart to sink in the strongest man surrounded, almost, by the deep, dark ocean, away from friends and relatives, the passengers and crew of the "May Flower," all landed, save one, on Plymouth's rock-bound shore. We cannot feel too grateful to God for having spared the lives of those worthy, fearless persons amid so much privation and danger. Kind reader, have you ever felt what it is to be on land or sea in this world and feel that you are alone. · If you have not, would that you may never experience it. And now, as these people had left their friends, never again in all probability to meet with them in this world, you can readily imagine what distress and sorrow must have filled their minds, and yet, for conscience sake, they were willing to give up all, to forsake all. A funeral at sea!

have you ever read of or witnessed one? If you have I need not remind you of its solemnity. During the long and tedious sailing on the restless ocean, but one death occured, only one was prevented by Divine Providence from reaching this country alive. One was also born on the wild ocean's breast, Peregrine White, and he landed with the rest. Sweet babe, the ocean bed was thy cradle, and the surging of the wild waves the first sound that thou didst hear. From that small beginning we are now a great and prosperous Nation.

What a remarkable example of God's fostering care does this land present. We now number over sixty million souls. When we think of it we are astonished beyond measure the increase has been so great and rapid. We have in this country every kind of soil and almost every kind of plant, animal and insect, and the variations of climate make it pleasant and agreeable to all. Surely, of a land to which so much is given, much will be required. Let us then be actively engaged in sending forth to the world everything that tends to elevate and benefit mankind. It is very pleasant after traveling on the ocean for a number of days, to see at length the "light-house" in the distance. Well, we predict that ere another hundred years shall have passed this country will have become the "Beacon Light" of the world, gleaming forth so that men can see in all directions, making steady advancement in everything calculated to benefit and ennoble the human race, proving the contrary to those who have so sneeringly asserted that a "Republic" cannot endure. A free Church and Ministry, entirely separate from state, is what we must ever approve. We need not fear a foreign foe, for we believe that we are strong enough (even with our poor coast defence) to repel an attempted invasion, coming from any source whatever. What we have most to guard against is internal strife and contention.

Our liberal principles of government, founded on religious toleration, have brought to our shores people of every creed and every nation, the worthy imigrant, as well as the nihilist and outcast; these conflicting elements have all to be dealt with firmly and judiciously. Never has there been more demand for christian and philanthropic efforts than for the past thirty years, and most nobly have our people

responded to the call, as may be attested from
the number and magnitude of our educational,
scientific, religious, and charitable institutions.
Neither have our efforts to benefit mankind
been confined within our own borders.   What
christian missionaries in any country have
shown greater zeal than our own in obeying
the Master's command, "Go ye into all the
world and preach the gospel?"   Our principles
of free government naturally incline us to
sympathize with the down-trodden of other
lands.   During the late persecutions of the
Christian Armenians by the blood-thirsty Mos-
lem, it remained for America to take the init-
iative step in aiding the helpless sufferers.
Whilst the other Christians stood aghast at
such wonderful cruelties, who but an American woman, and that our own noble Clara
Barton was the first to venture forth with aid
and comfort for the long suffering subjects of
a despotic government, and under the emblem
of that cross which even the fanatical Turk
was forced to respect.   We sincerely hope that
the day may soon come when all nations may
enjoy the same blessings that have been
granted us for so long a time, for when the rights

of the people are trampled on and not recognized in any way, then is unrest and upheaval, the powerful oppress the weak and the helpless are crushed to the earth, until at length, the cry goes up to Heaven "Oh Lord how long?" May we continue in the enjoyment of peace in this land, and ever move forward and upward in everything that is worthy and commendable, endeavoring to excel in every good word and work, and at length become what the Almighty assuredly designed we should be "the greatest land and people on earth."

My small book must now be brought to a close. In sending it forth I hope that it may be the means of shedding light on some disputed points in the life of my venerable neighbor, and highly esteemed friend, Mrs. Barbara Fritchie. I have stated facts in connection with her four-score years and over, which I hope may prove interesting to all. I have endeavored to impress on the youthful mind the importance of ever showing unswerving devotion to our beloved country. Nothing has been written in haste, or in an unkind, uncharitable spirit, but rather in the true spirit of harmony and love. That it may lead to kindlier and better feelings among those who have long been estranged is my sincere prayer. I have submitted the manuscript to the nearest relatives of Mrs. Fritchie now living, and after perusal they have stated to me that they believe it to be entirely correct and did not notice anything that should be changed.

I will here append a single statement of one of Mrs. Fritchie's relatives, Mrs. John H. Abbott, in substantiation of what I have stated. A large number of certificates are uncalled for or I could easily obtain and insert many. The statement from Mrs. Abbott to which I refer appeared in the Frederick News in July, 1897, and is as follows :

"Mrs. Abbott, as a grandniece of Whittier's heroine, is in possession of papers and articles once belonging to her famous relative, and also in a peculiar position to have first hand and accurate information of the facts in the case. Mrs. Abbott writes that Barbara Fritchie's signature of May, 1858, on business papers that passed between her and her business agent, when nearly 92 years of age, is remarkable as giving evidence of what she must have been able to do in earlier life.

"She was born in Pennsylvania, of German parentage, and may truthfully be called a German woman, but Mrs. Abbott states that she neither read or spoke the German language. As to her personal character, Mrs. Abbott says that her great-aunt was unostentatious and unassuming in manner, but of a highly refined nature. She had firmness and decision of character, also, when she believed herself in the right, but was ever gentle and sympathetic when occasion required. She was a woman of fine sensibilities, and fully alive to all that was transpiring around her.

" 'Her education,' Mrs. Abbott writes, 'was completed in the city of Baltimore, and was the best that could be obtained in her day. Not only was she fully able to write, but she was a thoroughly well read woman.' "

A

Description of Frederick City, Maryland.

FREDERICK CITY, MARYLAND.

BEAUTIFUL City of Frederick! Located in the lovely Monocacy valley, between the Catoctin mountain on the West, and the Sugar Loaf mountain on the East, wonder not that we love to stray among thy hills and valleys, for from 1745 when the village of Frederick was located, and named after "Frederick, Prince of Wales," her whole history has been of the most ennobling character. In the early history of this land, when oppressed by the mother country, the sons of Frederick City, and county, went forth with alacrity in her defense and when the demand was again made in 1775 for more soldiers, two companies were formed, and under command of Captain Michael Cresop and Captain Thomas Price, with John Ross Key as subordinate officer, (Father of Francis Scott Key) marched from Fredericktown to the camp at Boston to join Col. Washington. All demands ever made were most cheerfully responded to. The following highly important utterances were made by Fredericktown June 17, 1776: "That what may be re-

commended by a majority of the Congress,
equally delegated by the people of the United
Colonies we will at the hazard of our lives and
fortune support and maintain; and that every
resolution of the convention tending to separate this province from a majority of the Colonies, without the consent of the people, is de-
struction to our internal safety and big with
public ruin." On the 17th of January, 1781,
Gen. Morgan won a glorious victory over Tar-
leton at the Cowpens. It was in the pursuit
that followed this battle that the gallant Sargeant Everhart, of Frederick county, saved the
life of Col. Washington, at the head of the
Virginia cavalry. Many years after when Col.
Washington visited Frederick, he sent for his
old friend Everhart, and grasping his hand
embraced him. The meeting is said to have
been quite affecting. Sargeant Everhart was
one of the rescuers also of Lafayette from his
dangerous situation on the Brandywine. He died
in his 86th year within a few miles of Frederick. We were shown his sword, as well as
other military articles that belonged to him
whilst living, and had the pleasure of seeing
him before his death.

In the year 1777 barracks for the garrison of two batallions of infantry were erected in Frederick. The old buildings stood long upon the Southern suburbs of the town, and have now partially disappeared. The Deaf and Dumb Asylum stands on a portion of the site. They were used also to confine British prisoners of war. The old original log jail was also used for the same purpose. Afterward the barracks was used by the State of Maryland as an Armory, and the last use made of the buildings (prior to the Asylum taking charge of them,) was when the "Home Guard" of Frederick were guarding the City. The members would meet there and be sent in squads to guard the different sections of the City. They used first to meet at Coppersmith's Hall, corner of Market and Church streets, and were commanded by Gen. John A. Steiner, Captain Alfred Brengle, Captain Saunders and others at different periods. Here permit me to say that justice has never been done those men who traversed the streets of the City of Frederick, night after night with guns on their shoulders, and heavy ones they were, during the perilous times just preceeding the war.

We were glad to notice honorable mention made of them by Mr. Chas. W. Miller in his recently published "Directory and Business Guide." The position they occupied was perilous indeed. They were to see that nothing was brought into Frederick during the night intended to be conveyed to Virginia for the benefit of the enemy, and were provided with old, heavy guns to execute orders. One evening it was announced that a splendidly equiped military company was coming from Baltimore to pass over to Virginia. We asked Judge Nelson for instruction in regard to entering the City. We were informed that he stated we should allow them to enter, but not suffer them to tarry over night, but go directly on. In a short time they came and we marched them through the City to the suburbs, where, at the "Old Stone Tavern" they asked to get some refreshments, which was granted. We then marched them out to, and about half a mile down the Manor Lane, leading on to the Point of Rocks, when about to separate many of us thought a desperate struggle would ensue, as they were fully prepared and we had nothing but our old guns. We quickly fixed bayonets, depending more on this use of our guns than in firing for in that mode with their modern arms they had the decided advantage. It being nine or ten o'clock at night and somewhat dark they could not see well how poorly we were prepared to meet them. To our great surprise instead of turning on us and firing, they gave three hearty cheers to the Home Guard of Frederick.

On Prospect Hill, a short distance beyond where we turn into the Manor Lane, Col. Wm. P. Maulsby, now of Westminster, resided, and as we emerged from the lane that night, the Col. was waiting on horseback and invited us all up to his mansion, where tables ladened with every kind of refreshments were spread, and his estimable wife and daughter did all in their power to make all spend a sociable and pleasant time. When Gov. Hicks was in Frederick, the Home Guards were marching around where he was guarding the hotel the entire night. These are only a few of the incidents that occured during the time they served. Often those who were not on guard lay on the floor of the old barracks all night, without covering. They were presented by the ladies of Frederick with a splendid stand of colors. Hon. Reverdy Johnson, of Baltimore, made the presentation speech in the Court House yard.

We could give the names of those who were young men long ago, and went forth from Frederick in the Revolutionary war to battle for our common country, and came back, after enduring almost superhuman suffering, ruined in health, mere wrecks, having been as far North as Canada, and resting at night without shelter, yet they gladly endured it all for our glorious country. In the war of 1812 Frederick, including the county, again organized artillery and infantry companies and sent them speedily to the front, and in the late war of the Rebellion she sent forth many noble men to battle for the Union and a goodly number yielded up their lives in its defense. With sorrow we state that some of her sons on account of geographical location and family relationship, went into the Southern army.

Frederick was settled to a great extent by emigrants from Germany, and they proved to be hardy, industrious, christian people. They soon erected churches and school-houses. The

German language was spoken generally throughout the village, and the religious services in the churches were conducted in the same language. But the English as well as the German was taught in the day schools. One of the churches built, when Frederick could scarcely be called a town, yet stands, although built in the year 1763. It is the old German Reformed Church. True it was changed in the interior a few years since to adapt it to Sunday School purposes, but externally it has undergone but little change. Its noble lofty spire still points heavenward as in the days of yore, and the Town Clock in the steeple still announces to the inhabitants that time is rolling on. Many years ago, one Sabbath afternoon during a severe thunder storm, the steeple was struck by lightning but not severely impaired. The English members of the German Reformed sect in the year 1848 built on the opposite side of the street one of the most comfortable and beautiful churches in the State of Maryland. The old Evangelical Lutheran Church was partially removed some years ago and a very handsome and imposing new church, Gothic in style, erected in

front of where the old church stood. The bells
in the belfry of this church are peculiarly
sweet and plaintive in tone. We have traveled
considerably, but never heard any others of
exactly the same sound. They were, I believe,
cast in England and have considerable silver
in the composition. We have also a very costly Episcopal Church, the old original church
in the Queen Anne style of architecture being
used as a lecture room. The Methodist Episcopal congregation have also a fine new church;
the original church of Methodism was torn
down in the Summer of 1886 and now private
residences occupy the site. We have beside a
very neat and pretty Presbyterian Church. St.
John's Roman Catholic Church is large and
massive, finished in imitation of granite and
having in the steeple a chime of bells of as
sweet tone as found anywhere; also Trinity
Chapel, a second Methodist Episcopal Church;
a new brick church built by the United Breth-
ren, and a new, very substantial looking
church, built by the German Baptists. The
Salvation Army have built a large frame
church or barracks at the corner of Fourth and
Bentz streets. The colored people have two

large brick churches, and large congregations. The bells of the several churches we have named have called thousands together to worship in earthly sanctuaries, who are doubtless now singing Jehovah's praise around his throne in glory. The Court House is a very large and conveniently arranged brick building, located in a square surrounded by a grove of forest trees. The old, ancient looking Court House that occupied formerly the site of the present building, was a number of years since destroyed by fire. Here on the 28th of November, 1765, the first judicial decision was given against the constitutionality of the "Stamp Act." The Jail is a new and beautiful brick building, and stands where a few years since the old Jail stood, with its heavy iron barred windows and thick stone walls. Prior to the erection of the last building we had to depend for the security of prisoners on an old log Jail. The City Hall and Market House combined, are well worthy of notice. The lower, or first story is where the "Market" is held, and on a pretty Summer morning a stranger would be surprised to see the long line of wagons drawn up in front, and the large amount of every kind

of produce brought in from the rich surrounding county. The upper portion is used for the
Mayor's office. A large room is nicely fitted
up for this purpose, and back of it is a magnificent Hall, used for opera purposes, also for
political and social meetings. The old Market
House, which stood where the new one now
stands, was built in the year 1769. We have
a number of volunteer Fire Companies, with
elegant steam engines and everything required to do efficient work. We have a Young
Men's Bible Society, actively engaged in dis-
tributing God's Word; Young Men's Christian
Association; a Woman's Christian Temperance Union; Good Templars; Temple of Honor;
two lodges of Free Masons; the order of Odd
Fellows; Knights of Pythias; tribe of Red Men;
Knights of Honor; two white and one colored
army posts; two brass bands, the Frederick
City Cornet, which has acquired great reputa-
tion for discoursing splendid music, and Jen-
kins' Colored Cornet Band, which has been in
existence for many years. We can boast of a
number of well conducted hotels, the larger of
them being the City Hotel, Carlin House,
and Groff's. The Frederick Female Seminary

is well worthy of notice. It is now considered one of the leading Female Seminaries of the land. It is built in the Corinthian style of architecture, and is really beautiful, and has for its principal a most worthy christian gentleman of the highest intellectual culture, Prof. Joseph H. Apple. The Deaf and Dumb Asylum, built by the State of Maryland, was commenced in the year 1871 and is located here, and has a large attendance of scholars from all parts of the State. Its principal, Prof. Charles W. Ely, is a most estimable gentleman, and thoroughly qualified in every respect for the position. It occupies the most commanding site in the city. From the cupola you have a view of the county in every direction for a considerable distance. Its style of architecture is in the main Gothic, and wins the admiration of all beholders. We have also several Orphan Asylums, and a short distance from the city is Montevue Hospital, as fine a building as can be found anywhere for relieving and caring for the aged, the poor, the distressed. It is heated by steam and all the food furnished the inmates is such as any reasonable person might feel thankful to partake

of. Some years back, 1869, Mr. Louis Mc-
Murray, a capitalist, came here from Baltimore
City and established without asking the citizens
to take stock, or aid him in any way, a corn
canning establishment. He has gone on from
year to year putting up new buildings and increasing his facilities, until it has proven to be
a complete success, showing what enterprise
and capital can do. It is now one of the largest
houses engaged in the business in the United
States. In the regular canning season he
gives employment to eleven hundred hands,
and puts up, or fills as many sometimes as 150
thousand cans in a single day. Near the
Pennsylvania Railroad, on East street, Dr.
P. D. Fahrney conducts a large establishment
for the manufacture of the very best black ink,
and for the preparation of excellent medicines
known as the "Victor Remedies," for which he
has an extensive trade.

A hosiery factory has recently been
started in our midst by our citizens, and thus
far it appears as though it would prove quite
a success. We have a number of public and
private schools in the city, also the Frederick
City College, where, under able professors, a

good solid education can be obtained, and
where many men who have taken high rank
in literature and business circles were taught.
The Novitiate of the Catholic Church is an im-
mense educational institution where students
are in attendance from all sections of the Union. Though Frederick does not cover much
more territory than some years ago, yet it has
been greatly improved by tearing down old
buildings and placing in their stead new and
elegant private residences. The business men
have built many splendid store rooms, and
each of our banking institutions now transact
their business in new and beautiful buildings.
How different is this from over a hundred
years ago, 1745, when the town of Frederick
was laid out by an Englishman, and afterward
settled for the most part by worthy, industrious Germans. Then the streets were covered
with rows of wooden buildings, scarcely a brick
building to be seen. We have several planing
factories employing a number of hands; several
furniture establishments conducted on an extensive scale, and two foundries; three factories
where fertilizers are prepared to a large amount.
We also have within our corporate limits a

steam flour mill, where the very best flour is manufactured in large quantities, also the City flour mill, operated in the old way, located on Carroll creek, where excellent flour is made and furnished our citizens; several tanneries, where the best of leather is manufactured, and a number of establishments particularly along the banks of Carroll creek, where skins are dressed and gloves are made for wholesale and retail trade; some four or five coal yards, where every kind of coal is furnished, and we have several brick yards, where large quantities of brick are annually made and sold; also several extensive Coach factories, where the very best carriages of every kind are manufactured. A large number of useful and important inventions have emanated from citizens of Frederick, and in art we have artists of great ability, who fully deserve the recognition they have received. Frederick City is supplied with the very best and purest water brought from the neighboring mountains and we do not hesitate to state that purer water cannot be found in this or any other land. The scenery surrounding Frederick is of unsurpassed beauty, and is thus acknowledged to be by all unprejudiced persons. We have great wealth, and yet it is for the greater part in the hands of those advanced in years who have sufficient and do not care to embark in any enterprise however meritorious, hence our city in all these years has only grown from a village to a city of about ten thousand inhabitants. If Northern men of wealth and influence would settle among us, how different it would be. Why just think, within five miles of Frederick we have one of the loveliest points known to mortal man. It is White Rock, from the summit of which you have as lovely a view as is possible for the eye of man to rest upon, extending into Pennsylvania and Virginia, with springs of pure, ice cold water near, also springs strongly impregnated with iron and sulphur in the immediate vicinity. It could easily be made a delightful Summer resort, and yet nothing has been done to make it such to the present day. We have several railroads entering the city, making it quite easy of access and furnishing coal and lumber at reasonable rates. It was originally intended that the Baltimore and Ohio Railroad on its course westward should pass directly through Frederick, but on account of the

treachery of certain parties wielding considerable influence this purpose was frustrated, and
three miles east of Frederick at Monocacy
Junction its course was changed and a branch
only extended to our town.   The city of Frederick is not laid off as regularly, and the
streets are not as straight as you will find in
many other cities; particularly is this the case
with Patrick street, which would be the pret-
tiest street in the city, were it not for a considerable bend near the centre, which it is now
too late to remedy.   It is accounted for from
the fact that when the village was first located
the National pike leading westward ran in this
direction, and the surveying apparatus was
crude and imperfect, hence the result. Carroll
creek, a stream ordinarily low, but after heavy
continuous rains rising to a considerable
height, passes through the city, running east-
ward in its course until it reaches the Monocacy.   It is spanned by seven iron bridges in
its course through the city, entirely supplant-
ing the former old unsightly wooden structures.
We have moreover a beautiful cemetery,
Mount Olivet.   It is a precious place to visit,
for here repose not only the remains of our

friends and relatives, but many of Frederick's oldest and most respected citizens. Our city is remarkably healthy, as the health officers record will at any time show that the percentage of mortality is less according to the population than in most cities in the Union. We must acknowledge, however, that Frederick, notwithstanding its many natural advantages beauty of location and magnificent scenery, is not yet noted in business circles for energy and advancement and has not increased in population commensurate with the many advantages enjoyed. The Press of the city, consisting of three weekly and one daily paper, is ably conducted. The ability displayed in the editorials, the general selection and arrangement, would do full credit to any city. By means of telegraph and telephones in our midst we are enabled to communicate with all points with the greatest ease. Although Frederick has not increased so rapidly in population, it is and always will be a city of considerable importance, for it is surrounded by a county of the greatest fertility, producing almost every kind of grain and fruit and her agriculturists are men of enlarged views and highly intelligent